D0341516

The *Incredible* Search *for the* Treasure Ship *Atocha*

Brad Matsen

Enslow Publishers, Inc.

40 Industrial Road
Box 398
Berkeley Heights, NJ 07922
USA

PO Box 38
Aldershot
Hants GU12 6BP
UK

http://www.enslow.com

Library of Congress Cataloging-in-Publication Data

Matsen, Bradford.
 The incredible search for the treasure ship Atocha / Brad Matsen.
  p. cm. — (Incredible deep-sea adventures)
 Summary: Presents background information about the sinking of the Spanish
galleon, Atocha, in 1622 and describes efforts to locate the wreck and successfully
salvage its treasure more than 300 years later.
 Includes bibliographical references (p.   ) and index.
 ISBN 0–7660–2193–9 (hardcover)
 1. Nuestra Señora de Atocha (Ship)—Juvenile literature. 2. Treasure-trove—
Florida—Juvenile literature. 3. Shipwrecks—Florida—Juvenile literature. [1. Nuestra
Señora de Atocha (Ship) 2. Buried treasure. 3. Shipwrecks.] I. Title. II. Series:
Matsen, Bradford. Incredible deep-sea adventures.
 G530.N83 M39 2003
 909'.096348—dc21
                                        2002014311

Printed in the United States of America

10 9 8 7 6 5 4 3 2 1

To Our Readers: We have done our best to make sure all Internet Addresses in this book
were active and appropriate when we went to press. However, the author and the
publisher have no control over and assume no liability for the material available on those
Internet sites or on other Web sites they may link to. Any comments or suggestions can
be sent by e-mail to comments@enslow.com or to the address on the back cover.

Photo Credits: Photographs by Pat Clyne, Paradigm Productions, except where noted.
© 1999 Artville, LLC, p. 15; © Corel Corporation, p. 3; Yeorgos Lampathakis/National
Geographic Society Image Collection, p. 12; © Motivation, Inc., p. 31; © Motivation,
Inc. (Bill Muir, artist), p. 13.

Cover Photos: Photographs by Pat Clyne, Paradigm Productions.

Contents

ABOARD THE *DAUNTLESS*, MEL FISHER AND HIS CREW SEARCHED THE SEAS FOR THE HIDDEN TREASURE OF THE *ATOCHA*.

CHAPTER 1

Today's *the* Day

It is July 20, 1985, and the treasure-hunting boat *Dauntless* is anchored near some islands named the Marquesas Keys. The captain of the *Dauntless* is Kane Fisher. He and his crew are looking for the wreck of the Spanish ship named *Nuestra Señora de Atocha*. (The name means "Our Lady of Atocha.") The treasure ship has been on the bottom of the Gulf of Mexico since it sank during a hurricane in 1622.[1]

Aboard the *Dauntless*, the divers get ready for another day on the Gulf. Two of the crew, Andy Matroci and Greg Wareham, will scuba dive to search for silver, gold, and emeralds. They put on face masks, swim fins, and air tanks for breathing underwater.

Treasure divers have to be strong. They spend many hours every day underwater. They must also be very careful. Before they dive they check their equipment. Then they ask the other diver to check it, too. Everything must work perfectly.

Treasure divers are always hopeful. They know that every day could be the day they find the sunken treasure. Kane's father is Mel Fisher, the leader of the hunt for the *Atocha*. Mel Fisher's famous motto is "Today's the Day." It means that the treasure can be found on any day. He says that often, to keep everybody's spirits high while they search. His crews wear T-shirts with that motto on the front.[2]

Matroci and Wareham are excited as they get ready to dive. They wish each other good luck and jump into the ocean with a splash. The hunt is on.[3]

Searching on the Bottom

The water in the Gulf of Mexico is very beautiful. The deep water is purple. The shallow water is light blue. On this particular day Matroci and Wareham are diving in dark blue water about fifty-five feet (seventeen meters) deep. They swim down to the bottom and begin to search.

The water is not very clear in the place where Matroci and Wareham are searching. Currents and waves stir up the mud and sand from the bottom and make the water murky. First they swim in a straight line in one direction. Then they turn

THE BEAUTIFUL PURPLE AND BLUE WATER OF THE GULF OF MEXICO SURROUNDS THIS NATIONAL PARK NEAR THE FLORIDA KEYS.

around and swim back the other way. They make sure they look at everything below them.

Searching for sunken treasure is hard work. The gold, silver, cannons, swords, and other treasure from shipwrecks are not just lying around on the bottom in clear sight. They are buried in sand and mud. Searching divers only see a hint of treasure. The bottom is also covered with rocks, pieces of coral, crabs, and shells, so it can be hard to tell what is treasure and what is not.

On and on Matroci and Wareham search that morning. They can stay underwater for almost an hour with the air in their tanks. Then they have to come to the surface for new tanks. After making two or three dives, they will be replaced by other divers. All of Mel Fisher's divers hope they will be the ones to find the main treasure of the *Atocha*.

Clues About the Wreck

Some of the divers have already found traces of the *Atocha* and its treasure. Pieces of the ship were scattered around as it sank to the bottom. Mel Fisher and his crews have found some of *Atocha*'s cannons, some gold and silver coins, swords, and parts of the ship such as nails and anchors.

Mel and his divers found some of the clues to the location of the wreck of the *Atocha* on the bottom of the sea. They found other clues in books and records of the *Atocha*'s voyage, though. Those books and records say there is much more treasure to be found.[4]

Mel knows that the main part of the treasure is still somewhere on the bottom of the sea. He calls it the "mother lode." The artifacts his divers have already found are a trail he can follow. His search, however, has taken many wrong turns. For a long time, he followed what he thought was the right trail leading him into shallow water. But he did not find the main treasure.

Some of the people working with Mel on the *Atocha* treasure hunt are scientists called archaeologists. Archaeologists are people trained to decode the clues that are found in shipwrecks and other kinds of human ruins. During the sixteen years of the search, Mel and the archaeologists changed their minds several times about the location of the main wreck of the ship. They had come up with a new theory a few months before that morning in July 1985, when Matroci and Wareham made their dive. They now

MEL FISHER AND HISTORIAN EUGENE LYON STUDIED HISTORIC RECORDS OF *ATOCHA*'S VOYAGE, ITS CONSTRUCTION, AND THE SPANISH ATTEMPTS TO LOCATE THE TREASURE. THIS DOCUMENT IS A PAGE FROM *ATOCHA*'S LIST OF CARGO THAT INCLUDES IDENTIFYING MARKS FROM A SILVER BAR THAT WAS CARRIED ON THE SHIP.

THE TREASURE HUNTERS KNEW THAT THE GOLD
AND SILVER BARS FROM THE *ATOCHA* WOULD HAVE
IDENTIFIABLE MARKS STAMPED ON THEM.

thought the main treasure might not be in shallow water
where they have been looking for so long.[5]

So Kane Fisher and the rest of the crew of the *Dauntless*
are now searching in deeper water. From the books and
records, they have a good idea of what they will see
when they finally find the main wreck of the *Atocha*. They
know they will find stacks of silver coins. The coins will be
stuck together from being in the ocean for so long. The
chests that held the coins have rotted away during the 363
years the ship has been on the bottom.

They also know they will find silver bars. They are called
ingots. They will have special marks stamped on them. The
records of the *Atocha* have a list of the ingots and
those marks. They will be proof that they have found the
Atocha's treasure.

CHAPTER 2

The *Sinking* of the *Atocha*, 1622

Turn back the clock to September 4, 1622. On that day the *Nuestra Señora de Atocha* set sail for Spain carrying 400 million dollars in treasure. At the time, Spain was the most powerful country on earth. It sent ships all over the world to bring back treasure for its king.

The *Atocha* sailed from Havana, Cuba, with twenty-seven other ships. Some of the fleet were smaller merchant ships. They carried cargo such as sugar, spices, and cloth. Some were warships to guard the *Atocha* and her sister ship *Santa Margarita*, which was also carrying treasure.[1] *Atocha* and the other warships were heavily armed to protect them from the enemies of Spain at that time. The Dutch and English hoped to sink or capture Spanish ships such as the *Atocha* and take away the gold, silver, and jewels.

The Spanish Galleon

The *Atocha* was a kind of sailing ship called a galleon.[2] Galleons were the best, most modern ships of their time, the way modern battleships are now. The *Atocha* was 110 feet (34 meters) long, about as long as three school buses. It was 33 feet (10 meters) wide and its hull went 14 feet (4 meters) underwater. It had three tall masts for its big canvas sails. Some of the sails were square. Some went from the front mast to a long pole called a bowsprit that stuck out at the front of the ship. The *Atocha*'s bowsprit was 75 feet (23 meters) long.[3]

The *Atocha* and ships like it were the keys to the riches of the world for the king and merchants of Spain. Because they had the most powerful ships on earth, the Spanish were able to set up colonies in Florida, Mexico, and South America. Then they took the gold, silver, jewels, and other treasure from these places and shipped it back to Spain. With the treasure, they could afford to build more ships, set up more colonies, and get more treasure. The Spanish also used the treasure to pay for wars.

The *Atocha* was only two years old when it sailed from Havana that day in 1622. Its cargo holds were piled high with treasure. Its guns were ready for action. But it and the

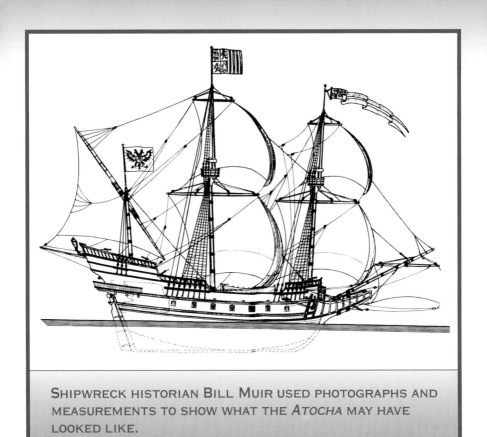

SHIPWRECK HISTORIAN BILL MUIR USED PHOTOGRAPHS AND MEASUREMENTS TO SHOW WHAT THE *ATOCHA* MAY HAVE LOOKED LIKE.

rest of the great Spanish fleet never reached the waiting enemy ships. The night after they sailed from Havana, a powerful hurricane screamed across the Gulf of Mexico. The mighty storm headed right for the *Atocha* and its twenty guard ships. It would become a day and a night of horror.

In the Teeth of a Hurricane

The hurricane began at dawn and the sky turned black with storm clouds and blowing water. Aboard the *Atocha*, crewmen climbed up the masts to take down the sails. The wind howled from the north. The sea crashed across the decks in huge green waves. At the end of the first day of the storm, the terrified sailors of the *Atocha* watched one of the smaller merchant ships sink. The *Nuestra Señora de la Consolaçion* capsized and disappeared with all its crew.[4]

Then the wind shifted and things got worse. Now the hurricane was blowing from the south. It was driving the treasure fleet into the reefs and shores of the Florida Keys. The Keys are a long string of islands that run from the bottom of mainland Florida into the Caribbean Sea like a fence of rock and coral. The Spanish sailors in the treasure fleet knew the Keys could be deadly to ships and they grew even more afraid.[5]

ON SEPTEMBER 4, 1622, THE *ATOCHA* MET WITH A POWERFUL HURRICANE. GIANT WAVES LIFTED THE SHIP, DROPPING IT ONTO A REEF. ONLY FIVE MEMBERS OF THE CREW SURVIVED.

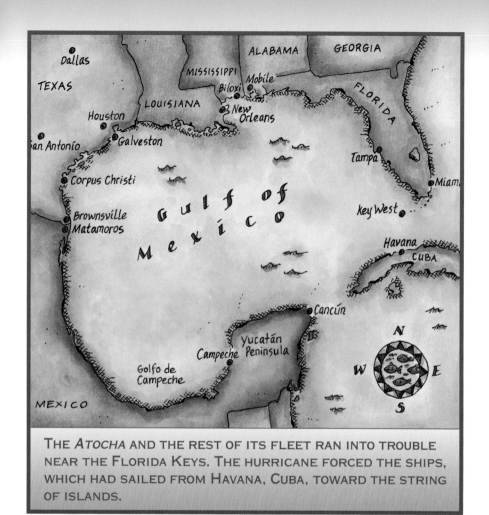

THE *ATOCHA* AND THE REST OF ITS FLEET RAN INTO TROUBLE NEAR THE FLORIDA KEYS. THE HURRICANE FORCED THE SHIPS, WHICH HAD SAILED FROM HAVANA, CUBA, TOWARD THE STRING OF ISLANDS.

By dawn of the second day, four or five ships were sunk. About twenty of the ships of the treasure fleet had been blown safely past the Keys. But the *Atocha* and *Santa Margarita* were doomed. They were still blowing right into the deadly shallow water of the Keys.

The crew and passengers of the *Atocha* huddled below deck and prayed. Their ship was out of control. It was heading straight for the reefs that lay between them and the safety of deep water. The sailors dropped anchors and hoped they could hold the *Atocha* off the reef. But the anchors did not hold.

A giant wave lifted the *Atocha* up and dropped it right down on top of the reef. Then another wave picked it up and threw it off the reef. Its hull broke into several pieces and the crew and passengers were scattered into the sea. Soon, the *Atocha* rested on the bottom in fifty-five feet of water. The tip of its tallest mast stuck up above the waves.

Five of the crewmen on the *Atocha* survived the wreck. They tied themselves to the rigging of the masts and were rescued the next day. Two hundred and sixty people drowned. The *Atocha* and the other lost ships of the treasure fleet were scattered for fifty miles (eighty kilometers) along the Keys.[6]

The First Search for the *Atocha*

The twenty ships that survived the hurricane went straight back to Havana and their captains reported the disaster. The nobles of Havana quickly sent five ships back to search for the *Atocha* and *Santa Margarita* and their treasures. They easily found the *Atocha* because its mast was still sticking above the water.

In those days, divers had no air tanks so they had to hold their breath when searching underwater for treasure. The *Atocha* was down at fifty-five feet, which was very deep for the divers. The treasure was locked in the cargo holds. The divers tried but could not hold their breath long enough to get to the treasure.[7]

THE TREASURES OF THE *SANTA MARGARITA* AND THE *ATOCHA* WERE LOST IN 1622. THIS IS SOME OF THE GOLD FROM THE *SANTA MARGARITA*.

Then, just a few weeks after the *Atocha* went down, another hurricane roared through the Caribbean Sea. The wreck of the ship was covered by sand and moved around on the bottom by the churning sea. The *Atocha* and its fabulous treasure disappeared for the next 363 years.

The
Nuestra Señora
de Atocha

Type of ship: Spanish galleon

Length: 110 feet (34 meters)

Width: 33 feet (10 meters)

Depth below water: 14 feet (4 meters)

Masts: 3

Year built: 1620

Year sunk: 1622

Passengers and crew: 265 (on the day it sank)

Survivors: 5

Value of treasure: $440 million (in 1985)

Kind of treasure: gold, silver, and jewels

CHAPTER 3

Mel Fisher's *Quest* for the Ghost Galleons

The *Atocha* and its fabulous treasure lay on the bottom of the ocean for more than three centuries. Many treasure hunters tried to find it and failed. They called the *Atocha* and *Santa Margarita* "The Ghost Galleons." Finally, in 1968, a man named Mel Fisher began his quest to find the wreck of the *Atocha* and its treasure.[1]

As a boy growing up in Indiana, Mel Fisher loved the ocean. He read *Treasure Island*, *Moby Dick*, and other adventure stories about the sea. When he was eleven, he built a diving helmet and pretended he was a deep-sea diver in lakes near his home. He dreamed of someday

MEL FISHER WAS INTERESTED IN THE OCEAN FROM THE TIME HE WAS A YOUNG BOY IN INDIANA. IN 1968 HE BEGAN HIS SEARCH FOR *ATOCHA*'S SUNKEN TREASURE.

really diving in the ocean. When he went to college, he studied to be an engineer but never forgot his dream of being an ocean diver.[2]

The Invention of the Aqua-Lung

When Mel Fisher was a young man, he heard about a new way of diving. Two French explorers, Jacques

Cousteau and Emile Gagnan, had invented the Aqua-Lung and scuba diving. (Scuba is short for *Self-c*ontained *u*nderwater *b*reathing *a*pparatus.) Now a diver could carry a tank of air on his or her back and breathe through a hose from the tank. This meant that a diver did not have to wear a heavy metal helmet and diving suit or be connected to the surface by a breathing hose. Fisher bought one of the very first Aqua-Lungs in the United States.

Fisher liked scuba diving so much he opened a store in California to sell Aqua-Lungs. He also sold the face masks,

SCUBA GEAR ALLOWS DIVERS TO CARRY A TANK OF AIR UNDERWATER. THE DIVER BREATHES THROUGH A HOSE FROM THE TANK.

swim fins, and other equipment that divers used. The new kind of diving became very popular. Mel Fisher was living his dream of diving in the ocean.[3]

Soon Fisher had a new dream. He wanted to use scuba diving to hunt for sunken treasure. In 1964, Fisher moved to Florida with his four children and his wife, Delores. Delores was also Fisher's business partner. The Fishers went to work with a treasure hunter named Kip Wagner. They found the wrecks of several ships that sank in 1715. They brought up more than 1,000 gold coins![4]

After they found their first ship, Mel and Delores Fisher were hooked on treasure hunting. They worked with Kip Wagner for a few years. Then the Fishers started their own treasure-hunting company. They named it "Treasure Salvors." Historians said the legendary wrecks of the *Nuestra Señora de Atocha* and *Santa Margarita* held millions of dollars worth of treasure. Mel Fisher's main goal was to find the Ghost Galleons of 1622.

Detective Work in Spain

First, Mel Fisher had to dig into the history of old Spanish shipwrecks to find the treasure. He became friends with a historian named Eugene Lyon. Lyon was a student at the University of Florida. He was studying the records of the early Spanish explorers, colonists, and their great fleets.

Fisher and Lyon agreed to work together to find the treasures of the *Atocha* and the *Santa Margarita*. Fisher went to Spain to look at the old, old records and maps of treasure

DELORES AND MEL FISHER, ALONG WITH EUGENE LYON (RIGHT), WORKED TOGETHER THROUGH THE YEARS TO FIND ATOCHA'S TREASURE. THEY WENT TO SPAIN TO CHECK OLD SHIP RECORDS AND MAPS. HERE, THEY ARE WEIGHING GOLD BARS RECOVERED FROM THE SANTA MARGARITA SITE.

voyages from the Caribbean Sea. Decoding those old records was harder than diving. The writing was blurry and faded. The language was hard to translate. Many of the maps made no sense at all. So Fisher asked Lyon to help him with his search. Since other treasure hunters were also looking for the *Atocha*, Fisher knew that he had to find it first to get the treasure.

Lyon had visited the records and maps in Spain several times. He went back again. This time, he discovered that the names on the maps were different 363 years ago. He figured out that the *Atocha* must be lying on the bottom of the sea near some islands now called the Marquesas Keys. Until then, nobody knew that. Lyon now thought the wreck must be a hundred miles from where the other treasure hunters were searching. Fisher believed him.[5]

The Marquesas Keys

The race to find the *Atocha* was on. Mel Fisher led his crew to the Marquesas. In the summer of 1970, he moved the headquarters of Treasure Salvors to Key West, Florida, which is only twenty miles from the Marquesas. The exact location of the wreck of the *Atocha* was still a mystery, but Eugene, Mel, and his divers thought they were on the right track.

To keep the search going, Mel had to raise a lot of money. At the office in Key West, he sold shares in the treasure hunt. Many people were very happy to invest money when Fisher told them that he was sure he could find a treasure that would be worth about half a billion dollars. The investors would divide the money from the treasure according to how much they gave Fisher.

And so the search began off the Marquesas. Mel Fisher and his crew used a boat named *Holly's Folly*. It had a special instrument that could detect metal on the bottom of the sea. The instrument is called a magnetometer. When the

TREASURE SALVORS, INC. MOVED TO KEY WEST, FLORIDA, TO CONTINUE THEIR SEARCH FOR *ATOCHA*'S TREASURE.

magnetometer showed that a big piece of metal was under the boat, divers would go down to check it out.[6]

Day after day, the crew of *Holly's Folly* dragged the magnetometer around near the Marquesas Keys. They found a crashed airplane from World War II. They found junk. They found fishing gear. But they found no sign of a Spanish shipwreck.

Searching for the *Atocha* had already cost about $200,000. Mel needed more money. He knew that to attract more investors, he had to find some proof that he knew what he was doing. He had to come up with a piece of the *Atocha* or the *Santa Margarita*. He also had to make his crews and investors believe he was going to find the treasure. Mel started using "Today's the Day" as his motto.[7]

The First Sign of the Ghost Galleons

Finally, on June 12, 1971, Captain Bob Holloway on *Holly's Folly* got lucky. He was searching in a new place, towing the magnetometer on the west side of the Marquesas. Bingo! There was a huge piece of metal below! Holloway put on his scuba gear and headed for the bottom. He thought he would find more junk or fishing gear. This time, however, he was wrong. There, on the bottom, was a giant anchor.

Mel Fisher went out to *Holly's Folly* to see for himself. He put on his own diving gear and swam down to the anchor. One look was all he needed. It was definitely an anchor from a Spanish galleon. There it was! A real galleon anchor. From the history books, he knew it came from the same period as the *Atocha* and *Santa Margarita*.[8]

Fisher left the anchor where it lay and a few days later brought back an underwater photographer to take a picture. He wanted to carefully record everything he found so archaeologists and historians such as Eugene Lyon could study it. Treasure in the ocean is very valuable but it is also important for teaching us about the past.

AN ARCHAEOLOGIST AND A DIVER MEASURE AND RECORD DRAWINGS OF THE ANCHOR THAT WAS FOUND ON JUNE 12, 1971. BUT WAS IT FROM THE *ATOCHA*?

The photographer, named Don Kincaid, swam down to take some pictures. He went down through a cloud of sand. There was the anchor. But suddenly, out of the corner of his eye, he saw the flash of something bright. There, to his surprise, was an eight-and-a-half-foot gold chain! Kincaid had found the first piece of gold from the Ghost Galleons.[9]

A Short Celebration

When they found the anchor and the gold chain, Fisher and his happy crew had a party aboard their boat. "To the *Atocha*," Mel said when he made a little speech that day. "Here's to the rest of all that loot—that $400 million—right down here. It's real close now. I can smell it."[10]

But Mel Fisher was not as close as he thought he was. He was pretty sure the anchor and gold chain were from the Ghost Galleons, but where was the rest of the *Atocha* and *Santa Margarita*?

They continued to find signs of shipwrecks. They found muskets, swords, cannon balls, and pieces of old sailing ships. But they did not find the *Atocha* or the *Santa Margarita*.

These were hard times for Mel Fisher and his crews. They spent many long days diving. The search cost thousands and thousands of dollars. Still, they did not find the ships. And worse, the other treasure hunters figured out that Mel might be on the trail of the Ghost Galleons and came to the Marquesas Keys. They would not search exactly where Fisher's divers were, but they hunted nearby. The first divers to find the wreck would become the owners of the treasure. The stakes were enormous.

"Today's the day," Mel said, over and over. "Today's the day." And most of his divers, crews, friends, family, and investors continued to believe that he would find the lost ships and their fortune in gold, silver, and jewels.

CHAPTER 4

The *Search* Goes *On* and *On*

K ane Fisher, his father Mel Fisher, and their loyal crew members continued the search for the wreck of the *Atocha*. It was a great quest that began when Mel Fisher read about the sinking of the *Atocha* and her fabulous treasure. When Mel started hunting, he never expected it would take so long to find the wreck. He never expected the entire search would have a final cost of millions of dollars.

After the divers found the big anchor and the gold chain, they found nothing for almost two years. By 1975, the treasure hunters had been searching for seven years. Finally, they found fragments of ships and treasure. The trail seemed to lead to deeper water.[1]

GOLD BARS AND DISKS WERE FOUND ALONG THE *ATOCHA* TRAIL.

The Mailbox

Searching for treasure underwater is hard work. When divers found a trace of a wreck or a piece of treasure, they would dig in the mud, rock, and sand around their discovery. They used a new invention to dig up the bottom.

Before he started looking for the *Atocha*, Mel started using what he called a "mailbox" to help the search on the bottom. The mailbox was invented by his friend, Fay Fields. A mailbox was a big tube that blew water down to help dig up the bottom. The tube was attached to the back of a boat near the propellers. When the divers were searching below, the crew on the boat ran the engines, turning the propellers. The force of the water moving down through the mailbox made digging much easier.[2]

Mel's son Dirk Fisher was the captain of the *Northwind*, one of the treasure hunting boats in 1975. The *Northwind* had very big propellers and the mailboxes worked really well. Dirk was a strong believer in the idea that the wreck of the *Atocha* was in even deeper water, so he took the *Northwind* to search there.

On July 13, 1975, Dirk Fisher found five of the *Atocha*'s cannons! Then he and his crew began digging with the mailbox and soon

THIS SKETCH SHOWS HOW THE MAILBOX'S LARGE TUBE BLEW WATER TO THE BOTTOM OF THE SEA. THE FORCE OF THE WATER HELPED DIVERS DIG FOR TREASURE.

uncovered four more. The cannons were beautiful. They were made of bronze. The coat of arms of the Spanish king was marked on each one of them. The cannons were decorated with images of dolphins. They knew the cannons were from the *Atocha* because the records in Spain described them exactly.[3]

THESE MAILBOXES ARE READY FOR USE TO HELP THE TREASURE HUNTERS ON THE SEAFLOOR.

Though the discovery of the cannons made everybody very happy, there were still big questions with no answers. Did the cannons fall off the *Atocha* before it sank? Did they sink to the bottom much faster than the wood of the ship and therefore end up far away from the main wreck? After they found the cannons, the trail to the *Atocha* seemed to be lost.

The *Northwind* Sinks

And then disaster struck. On the night of July 20, 1975, the *Northwind* was anchored in the still water off the

Marquesas. Captain Dirk Fisher, his wife Angel, photographer Don Kincaid, and their crew members had a small party to celebrate Angel's birthday. That night, they talked about the discovery of the cannons and how they were sure *Atocha*'s main treasure was nearby. Tomorrow might really be "The Day." Then they all went to sleep.

Just before dawn, the *Northwind* capsized and sank to the bottom. Don Kincaid and six of the crew were thrown clear of the doomed boat. Dirk, Angel, and a new diver named Rick Gage were lost at sea. This tragedy struck Mel Fisher and his wife Delores like a thunderbolt. Everyone who worked for Treasure Salvors was devastated.[4]

"A tragedy as regrettable as this can sometimes divide a company," said Duncan Mathewson, an archaeologist. "But the deaths of Dirk, Angel, and Rick seemed to bring all of us closer together. The loss of human lives made my commitment to finding the *Atocha* all the more important. I couldn't abandon her now."[5]

Like Dirk Fisher, Duncan Mathewson was convinced that the wreck of the *Atocha* was in even deeper water. But some of Mel's divers continued to look in shallower water. Five years after Dirk found the *Atocha*'s cannons, those divers dug up some pottery, clumps of silver coins, and three solid gold bars. Treasure! Could this be the *Atocha*?

The Wreck of the *Santa Margarita*

The treasure was not from the *Atocha*. Mel Fisher had found the wreck of the *Santa Margarita*. Because of

TRAGEDY STRUCK THE TREASURE TEAM WHEN DIRK FISHER AND HIS WIFE ANGEL WERE KILLED WHEN THEIR *NORTHWIND* BOAT SANK.

the numbers on the gold, Eugene Lyon knew they came from the other Ghost Galleon. Eventually, Treasure Salvors would recover gold, silver, jewels, and artifacts worth more than $50 million from the *Santa Margarita*. But the mystery deepened. Where was the wreck of the *Atocha*?

According to the records of the survivors, the *Santa Margarita* had gone down three miles or more from the *Atocha*. Mel Fisher left some crews there to salvage its treasure. Then he turned his attention again to finding the great treasure of the *Atocha*.

Hawk Channel and Deeper Water

For five more years Mel Fisher and his divers searched. Kane Fisher, one of Mel's other sons, became the captain of his own boat, the *Dauntless*. Like Dirk, Duncan Mathewson, and other crew members, Kane was convinced that the *Atocha* was in deeper water, in a place called Hawk Channel.

KANE FISHER HOLDS SOME OF THE JEWELRY AND EMERALDS HE FOUND. IT WASN'T THE WHOLE TREASURE, BUT THE TEAM WAS GETTING CLOSE!

For three years, until 1985, Kane Fisher and the *Dauntless* followed the trail out into Hawk Channel. They found nails, barrel hoops, spikes, and hunks of rock called ballast. And then one of the crew, Susan Nelson, found 13 gold bars, 414 silver coins, and 4 pieces of jewelry with 16 emeralds. It was not the great treasure, but Dirk's deep water theory was beginning to make sense to Mel and the rest of the divers and experts of Treasure Salvors.

The Treasure of the *Atocha*

It is the morning of July 20, 1985. The divers from the *Dauntless*, Andy Matroci and Greg Wareham, peer through the murky water. For awhile they see only rocks, shells, sand, and mud. Then, through the cloudy water, they spot what looks like a black reef right ahead of them. The excited divers swim to the reef. As they get closer, they can hardly believe their eyes. It is not a reef. It is a mountain of real silver bars neatly stacked on the bottom of the ocean. They also see stacks of coins.

Matroci and Wareham have found the great treasure of the *Nuestra Señora de Atocha*!

Captain Kane Fisher and his crew on the *Dauntless* see Matroci and Wareham pop to the surface. The divers shout that they have found the *Atocha*'s treasure. Kane picks up his radio microphone. He calls Mel Fisher's office in Key West, Florida. He tells him the great news.

"Put away the charts," Kane says. "We found it."[6]

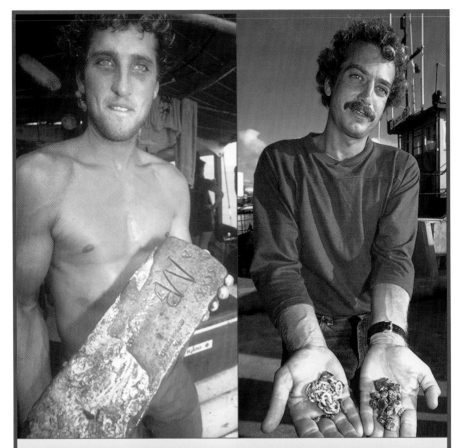

DIVERS GREG WAREHAM (LEFT) AND ANDY MATROCI WERE LUCKY ENOUGH TO BE THE DIVERS THE DAY THE *ATOCHA* TREASURE WAS DISCOVERED. WAREHAM HOLDS AN ENORMOUS SILVER BAR AND MATROCI DISPLAYS SOME OF *ATOCHA*'S JEWELS.

After sixteen long years, the search is over. The gold, silver, jewels, and artifacts of the *Atocha* will be worth $440 million. And Mel Fisher's dream has come true. He is the greatest treasure hunter of all time.

MEL FISHER AND HIS CREW CELEBRATE THE SUCCESSFUL END OF THEIR SIXTEEN YEAR TREASURE HUNT. *ATOCHA*'S TREASURE HAD BEEN FOUND.

NEWS PHOTOGRAPHERS, WHO WOULD BE WAITING ON THE DOCKS WHEN THE BOATS CAME IN, DOCUMENT THE FIND OF EMERALDS FROM *ATOCHA*.

MEL FISHER'S SON
KIM FISHER ▶

...IVER, WEARING A "TODAY'S
...E DAY" SHIRT, SHOWS OFF
...ME OF THE EMERALDS FROM
...E *ATOCHA* SITE. ▼

THESE BEAUTIFUL GOLD LINKS
WERE PART OF A JEWELED BELT.
EVERY LINK CONTAINED
DIFFERENT GEMS, SUCH AS
PEARLS, RUBIES, AND DIAMONDS.

CHAPTER 5

Atocha's Treasure Is *Worth* More Than *Money*

Mel Fisher and his crews had a big party in Key West to celebrate the discovery of the *Atocha*. Then they went to work bringing up the treasure. That job would last for years. Before bringing up the gold, silver, jewels, and artifacts, the crews recorded where each piece lay on the bottom.

This was very important to archaeologists and historians to whom the wreck of the *Atocha* is a time machine. From the ancient ship they would learn how people lived 363 years before. To them, this knowledge is even more valuable than money. It is priceless.[1]

ARCHAEOLOGIST DUNCAN MATHEWSON HOLDS A GOLD CHAIN AND GOLD BARS—MORE TREASURE FROM THE GHOST GALLEON *ATOCHA*. NOTICE THE GRID ON THE OCEAN FLOOR.

The divers carefully divided the site of the wreck into a grid pattern. Each part of the grid was numbered. That way they could keep track of each piece of the ship and its treasure. On land, archaeologists then drew charts, maps, and diagrams of the site and came up with a very good picture of the *Atocha* on the day it went down in the hurricane.[2]

See the Treasure of the *Atocha* Today

Mel Fisher divided up the treasure. He gave some to his investors, his crews, and other Treasure Salvors workers. Some of them sold their shares of the treasure. Some kept them. And some gave the treasure to museums so other people could see it, too.

Mel and Delores Fisher gave part of their share of the treasure to a museum. It is now on display in the Mel Fisher Maritime Heritage Museum in Key West, Florida. There, you can see the fabulous jewels, gold chains, swords, navigation instruments, silver ingots, emeralds, and the rest of the treasure Fisher and his crews found. You can also see exhibits that tell the story of Mel Fisher, his dream, and sixteen years of searching for the lost treasure of the *Nuestra Señora de Atocha*.[3]

And you can dream of treasure hunting yourself.

Chapter Notes

CHAPTER 1. TODAY'S THE DAY

1. R. Duncan Mathewson III, *Treasure of the Atocha* (New York: E.P. Dutton, 1986), p. 14.

2. *The Atocha*, n.d., <http://www.ocf.berkeley.edu/~mars> (February 23, 2002).

3. Ibid.

4. Mathewson, pp. 64–69.

5. Ibid.

CHAPTER 2. THE SINKING OF THE *ATOCHA*, 1622

1. R. Duncan Mathewson III, *Treasure of the Atocha* (New York: E.P. Dutton, 1986), pp. 23–24.

2. Robert Daley, *Treasure: The Story of the Most Successful and Most Tragic Treasure Hunt of Modern Times* (New York: Random House, 1977), pp. 21–22.

3. Eugene Lyon, *The Search for the Atocha* (New York: Harper and Row, 1979), pp. 45–46.

4. Mathewson, pp. 23–24.

5. Ibid.

6. Ibid.

7. Daley, pp. 30–33.

CHAPTER 3. MEL FISHER'S QUEST FOR THE GHOST GALLEONS

1. R. Duncan Mathewson III, *Treasure of the Atocha* (New York: E.P. Dutton, 1986), pp. 32–33.

2. *The Atocha*, n.d., <http://www.ocf.berkeley.edu/~mars> (February 23, 2002).

3. Robert Daley, *Treasure: The Story of the Most Successful and Most Tragic Treasure Hunt of Modern Times* (New York: Random House, 1977), pp. 41–45.

4. *The Atocha*.

5. Mathewson, pp. 33–35.

6. Ibid., pp. 35–37.

7. *The Atocha*.

8. Mathewson, pp. 35–37.

9. Ibid., pp. 33–35.

10. Ibid., p. 36.

CHAPTER 4. THE SEARCH GOES ON AND ON

1. R. Duncan Mathewson III, *Treasure of the Atocha* (New York: E.P. Dutton, 1986), pp. 70–73.

2. *The Atocha*, n.d., <http://www.ocf.berkeley.edu/~mars> (February 23, 2002).

3. Eugene Lyon, *The Search for the Atocha* (New York: Harper and Row, 1979), pp. 171–173.

4. Mathewson, p. 78.

5. Ibid.

6. Ibid., p. 14.

CHAPTER 5. *ATOCHA*'S TREASURE IS WORTH MORE THAN MONEY

1. Eugene Lyon, *The Search for the Atocha* (New York: Harper and Row, 1979), pp. 171–178.

2. Ibid.

3. *Mel Fisher Maritime Heritage Society*, "Exhibitions," © 2001, <http://www.melfisher.org/1622.htm> (June 9, 2002).

Glossary

Aqua-Lung—A tank and breathing hose for diving underwater.

archaeologist—A person trained to interpret history by looking at treasure, ruins, and other evidence of humans.

artifact—A sword, suit of armor, cannon, or other object made by humans that gives clues to life in the past.

astrolabe—An instrument for navigating by the stars.

ballast—Rocks and other material used to increase the weight of a ship to make it more seaworthy.

bowsprit—A long timber for holding sails on a ship's front.

galleon—A type of sailing ship built in the 1600s that was very fast and heavily armed with cannons.

grid—A pattern for searching on the bottom of the sea and recording what is there.

magnetometer—An electronic instrument for detecting metal underwater.

mast—A tall timber that rises from the deck of a sailing ship on which the sails hang.

rigging—Ropes and ladders from the deck to the masts of sailing ships.

salvor—A person or ship that hunts for wrecks and treasure.

scuba—Self-contained *u*nderwater *b*reathing *a*pparatus. Allows divers to swim underwater to depths of about two hundred feet using tanks of air carried on their backs.

Further Reading

BOOKS

Barber, Nicola, and Anita Ganeri. *The Search for Sunken Treasure*. New York: Raintree Steck-Vaughn Publishers, 1997.

Gibbons, Gail. *Sunken Treasure*. New York: HarperCollins, 1999.

Pickford, Nigel. *Atlas of Shipwrecks & Treasure*. New York: DK Publishing, Inc., 1994.

Reid, Struan. *The Children's Atlas of Lost Treasures*. Brookfield, Conn.: Millbrook Press, 1997.

Schwartz, Alvin. *Gold and Silver, Silver and Gold: Tales of Hidden Treasure*. New York: Farrar, Straus and Giroux, 1993.

INTERNET ADDRESSES

The Atocha. <http://www.ocf.berkeley.edu/~mars/>.

McHaley, Bleth, and Wendy Tucker. *Treasure Net*. "The Mel Fisher Story." <http://www.treasurenet.com/found/melfisher>.

Mel Fisher Maritime Heritage Society. ©2001. <http://www.melfisher.org>.

Index